Original title:
Mossy Glimmers Under the Unicorn Hem

Copyright © 2025 Swan Charm
All rights reserved.

Author: Sebastian Sarapuu
ISBN HARDBACK: 978-1-80559-425-3
ISBN PAPERBACK: 978-1-80559-924-1

Whims of the Forest's Heart

Among the trees where whispers dwell,
A secret world begins to swell.
The sun breaks through with warm caress,
Inviting all to seek its bless.

Each leaf a note in nature's song,
The melodies where spirits throng.
Dancing shadows cast by light,
A tapestry of day and night.

Footsteps soft on mossy ground,
In this retreat, peace can be found.
Ferns unfurl in emerald grace,
In this stillness, time finds its place.

The breeze carries a tale of old,
Of creatures brave and hearts so bold.
In every nook, a story waits,
For those who dare unlock the gates.

With every breath, the forest sighs,
A symphony beneath the skies.
In sunlight's glow and moonlit art,
We find the whims of the forest's heart.

Under the Gaze of Ethereal Light

In twilight's hush, the stars awake,
Each glowing orb a path to take.
Soft whispers drift on silver streams,
Where every glance fulfills a dream.

Beneath the boughs of ancient trees,
The air is filled with sacred pleas.
A dance of shadows, light entwined,
In this realm, no joy confined.

Moonbeams weave a cloth of grace,
Embracing all in their warm embrace.
The night sings sweet and tender lull,
As hearts unite, the world feels full.

In every glimmer, secrets hide,
Under the gaze, we cast aside.
The burdens of the day are tossed,
In celestial dreams, we are embossed.

So let the stars guide us tonight,
Into the depths of cosmic light.
Together, we'll let our spirits soar,
Under the gaze of forevermore.

Dreamscapes in Lush Embrace

In fields adorned with flowers bright,
We wander free in soft daylight.
Each petal paints a canvas true,
A world where all our dreams break through.

The gentle hum of nature calls,
As golden light through foliage falls.
In every corner, wonders bloom,
Creating magic, lifting gloom.

We chase the butterflies in flight,
Their delicate dance, a pure delight.
Amongst the tall and swaying grass,
We find a peace that's meant to last.

With laughter ringing through the air,
Our spirits lift, we breathe the fair.
In every glance, a tale unfolds,
In dreamscapes where our hearts are bold.

So let us tread this vibrant land,
With open hearts and willing hands.
In lush embrace, we'll find our way,
Through dreamscapes bright as night meets day.

Cradled by the Mirth of Nature

In morning's light, the world awakes,
With every sound, a joy that breaks.
The rustling leaves in playful dance,
Invite us all to join the chance.

With giggles soft and laughter free,
Nature sings its melody.
Each creature plays its part in cheer,
As sunshine weaves its golden sphere.

Through valleys deep and mountains high,
The heart of earth begins to sigh.
Cradled in the arms of trees,
We find our solace in the breeze.

In every stream, a story flows,
A journey told as friendship grows.
Each moment shared, a treasure found,
In nature's joy, our hearts are bound.

So let us revel in the play,
Embraced by earth, come what may.
For in the mirth, we are alive,
In nature's arms, we thrive and strive.

Celestial Dreams in the Embrace of Foliage

In the forest's gentle hug,
Stars whisper through the leaves.
Moonlight dances on the ground,
Where every shadow weaves.

Crickets sing their twilight song,
While breezes softly sway.
Dreams take flight on wings of hope,
In the night's soft ballet.

The canopy a vaulted dome,
Cradling dreams that gleam.
Branches twirl in silent grace,
As starlit visions stream.

Every rustle tells a tale,
Of whispers from above.
In this sacred, leafy realm,
The heart learns how to love.

As dawn breaks through the shrouded veil,
New beginnings glow.
Through foliage, dreams remain,
In the light's warm flow.

Vibrations of Magic in Autumn's Embrace

Leaves of amber swirl around,
As brisk winds twist and play.
Nature's palette paints the trees,
In a fiery display.

Beneath the boughs, time slows down,
With every breath, I feel.
The touch of magic in the air,
Autumn's soft appeal.

Pumpkins grin from every step,
The harvest sings its tune.
Crisp air whispers ancient spells,
Underneath the silver moon.

Each leaf a note in nature's song,
An orchestra of change.
The world around is alive and bright,
In this dance so strange.

With every sunset, colors blend,
And dreams begin to soar.
In autumn's warm embrace I find,
A magic I adore.

Hidden Stories of Moonlit Lace

Underneath the silver veil,
Where shadows twist and glide,
Moonlit lace weaves delicate tales,
Of secrets deep and wide.

Each thread a whisper of the night,
Each stitch a dream's soft sigh.
The cosmos twinkles in delight,
As stars flicker and fly.

Through cobwebs of forgotten roads,
Ancient echoes dance.
The night holds stories yet untold,
In a fleeting glance.

Twilight weaves its gentle craft,
In patterns made of light.
Hidden treasures come alive,
In the velvet night.

As dawn approaches, moments fade,
Yet memories hold fast.
In moonlit lace, we find the time,
In shadows, dreams are cast.

Echoing Laughter in the Sapphire Night

Beneath the starlit sapphire sky,
Laughter rings like chimes.
Echoes dance through open fields,
In playful, merry rhymes.

Each giggle floats on gentle waves,
Of soft and breezy air.
Night's embrace holds joy in thrall,
A symphony to share.

The moon grins down with tender light,
As friendships intertwine.
In the quiet moments linger,
Where hearts are pure and fine.

Every whisper mingles with the breeze,
Painting worlds anew.
In laughter's balm, our souls unite,
As dreams begin to brew.

The night a canvas, deep and wide,
Where joy paints every thought.
Echoing laughter fills the space,
With every joy we sought.

Crystal Dewdrops on Forgotten Paths

Crystal dewdrops glisten bright,
On paths that fade from human sight.
Whispers of the morning air,
Nature breathes without a care.

Ferns and moss weave tales untold,
In sunlight's grasp, a hue of gold.
Each step echoes history's song,
In silence, where the lost belong.

Winding trails of emerald hue,
Show secrets buried, old yet new.
In the stillness, dreams lay bare,
Prepared to wander, hearts laid bare.

Beneath the shade of ancient trees,
The scent of pine floats on the breeze.
Every droplet tells a tale,
Of wanderers who sought the trail.

When twilight falls, the shadows blend,
The paths still call; the journey's end.
With crystal dewdrops in the light,
Lost souls find peace in the night.

Celestial Petals in the Twilight Mist

Celestial petals drift and swirl,
In twilight's grip, a magic unfurl.
Colors blend in soft embrace,
Nature's canvas, a tranquil space.

Misty dreams weave through the air,
Perfumed whispers, scents so rare.
Dancing lightly on the breeze,
Every petal brings heart's ease.

Stars awaken in the hush,
As blooms unfold in evening's blush.
Under moonlight's silver stream,
The world reflects a gentle dream.

In gardens where the shadows play,
Each petal holds the end of day.
A symphony in hues of night,
Crafted in the softest light.

Celestial whispers softly sound,
In the twilight, beauty's found.
Petals drift on quiet paths,
Of love and hope, and gentle laughs.

Radiance of the Whispering Woodlands

Radiance glows in woodlands deep,
Where ancient secrets safely sleep.
Sunbeams filter through the leaves,
Eternal tales the forest weaves.

Whispers echo in the trees,
The rustling dance of summer's breeze.
Gentle laughter, nature's voice,
In every shadow, life rejoice.

Mushrooms peek from nature's floor,
While creatures scurry to explore.
The heartbeats of the woodland hum,
In harmony, they all become.

Rays of sunlight paint the ground,
In this haven, peace is found.
The woodlands breathe, alive and free,
A sanctuary for you and me.

As twilight drapes its silken veil,
The magic grows; our dreams set sail.
Radiance in every leaf and vine,
In the whispering woods, we align.

Guardians of the Glimmering Hollow

Guardians watch in silence here,
In the glimmering hollow, clear.
With eyes like stars, they hold the night,
Protectors of all that is bright.

Mossy stones beneath their feet,
Ancient wisdom, gifts discreet.
Each flicker of light a tale,
Of time that passes, soft and frail.

In shadows deep, their spirits soar,
Whispered promises of yore.
Oaths to guard the dreams we weave,
To cherish what we dare believe.

When dawn approaches, hope's own spark,
The guardians dwell, yet leave their mark.
In every glint, in every glow,
The magic of the hollow flows.

As twilight bids the world goodbye,
Their watchful gaze will never die.
With every star that starts to shine,
Guardians keep the dreams divine.

Enchanted Souls Beneath the Quiet Canopy

In the hush of evening light,
Whispers dance through leaves so bright.
Shadows cradle dreams anew,
Where magic sparks in every hue.

Two hearts wander, hand in hand,
In this ethereal, timeless land.
Laughter floats on gentle sighs,
As stars emerge in velvet skies.

The breeze carries tales of old,
Of secrets shared, and love retold.
Underneath this tranquil dome,
Souls entwined have found their home.

Moments weave a tapestry,
Of joy, of love, of harmony.
In nature's lap, they heal and grow,
Beneath the trees, their spirits glow.

As night unfolds its starry cloak,
They share their dreams, the words bespoke.
In silence deep, their hearts connect,
In the canopy, they find respect.

Traces of Wonder in Twilight's Hold

As daylight fades to dusky grace,
The world transforms, a sacred space.
Soft hues blend in tender light,
Revealing wonders of the night.

Footprints linger on this path,
Leading to the moon's soft bath.
Glimmers spark in lovers' eyes,
As magic weaves through cosmic ties.

The air is thick with whispered dreams,
As the twilight softly gleams.
Every star a tale to tell,
In this serene and mystic spell.

A symphony of night unfolds,
Each note a secret that it holds.
In shadows deep, their laughter rings,
A melody of ancient things.

And in the quiet, hearts ignite,
Chasing whispers of the night.
In every pause, a chance to see,
The traces of sweet mystery.

Dappled Dreams Beneath Endless Skies

In fields where sunlight gently spills,
Nature breathes, and quiet thrills.
Dappled dreams in colors blend,
Where every moment holds a friend.

The breeze, a gentle serenade,
Invites the soul to dance unmade.
Where flowers nod in soft reply,
Underneath the vast, blue sky.

Each petal holds a wiild surprise,
Beauty dwells in nature's eyes.
The horizon stretches far and wide,
As dreams awaken, hearts collide.

Laughter echoes through the ways,
In this Eden of sunlit days.
Together in the golden glow,
They breathe in life, with joy they flow.

With every step, the world unspools,
As they weave through dappled pools.
In nature's hand, they find their place,
Embraced by warmth and soft embrace.

A Tapestry of Blooms Under Star-kissed Boughs

In gardens rich with colors bright,
Nature crafts a pure delight.
Petals whisper soft and low,
As evening's breath begins to blow.

Stars blink down in gentle awe,
Gifting dreams that leave us raw.
In every bloom, a story starts,
A tale embedded in our hearts.

Under boughs that bow and weave,
We find the bliss that we believe.
The night unravels, soft and kind,
As secrets of the heart unwind.

A tapestry of hues and scents,
In nature's arms, where love repents.
Joy spills forth in every hue,
As hearts entwine, the old and new.

Beneath the stars, they share their dreams,
In quiet moments, love redeems.
A dance of blooms, a breathless sigh,
Underneath the vast, dark sky.

The Dance of Light in Fern-clad Hollows

In the hush of twilight's embrace,
Golden rays weave through the green,
Fern-clad hollows softly glow,
Nature's stage, a tranquil scene.

Leaves sway gently, a graceful tune,
Echoes of whispers drift through the air,
Sunset's brush paints shadows long,
In the dance of light, none can compare.

Glow of fireflies begins to spark,
Guiding hearts to forgotten paths,
Underneath the stars that mark,
The silent joy that nature hath.

The cool breeze stirs the dormant night,
Every flicker brings tales untold,
In this magic, where dreams take flight,
The fern-clad hollows, a sight to behold.

A Serenade of Whispering Leaves

In the breeze, the leaves converse,
A symphony of soft, sweet sighs,
Rustling gently as the day fades,
Underneath the vast, starlit skies.

Each branch tells a story old,
Whispers carried on the wind,
Tales of seasons, brave and bold,
In the twilight, where dreams begin.

Moonlight glimmers on dew-kissed veins,
Nature's notes, a melodic call,
In the silence, beauty reigns,
A serenade, enchanting all.

Together they sway, a waltz divine,
Amidst the shadows, they gently weave,
In the heart of night, their voices align,
Within the forest, they shan't leave.

Phantoms of the Meadow at Dusk

As daylight dips, the shadows grow,
Meadows whisper secrets low,
Phantoms drift through golden haze,
In dusk's embrace, they find their ways.

Flickers of movement, soft and light,
Ghostly figures in fading sight,
A dance of memories on the glade,
Where time itself begins to fade.

The crickets serenade the night,
Their songs entwine with fading light,
Grass sways gently to the tune,
Underneath the watchful moon.

In the quiet, magic stirs,
Whispers of dreams, the heart prefers,
Phantoms linger, secrets keep,
In the meadow's arms, they sleep.

Crystal Dew on Whispered Secrets

Morning breaks with a tender glow,
Crystal dew, like diamonds, show,
Each drop a secret held so dear,
Whispers of night, so soft and clear.

Leaves adorned in silken threads,
Nature's jewels, where silence spreads,
A tapestry of light, so rare,
Awakens dreams, floating in air.

As sunlight spills, the world ignites,
Every petal, an artist's delight,
Whispered secrets of tranquil streams,
Reflect the beauty of waking dreams.

In this moment, time stands still,
Crystal dew wrapped with gentle thrill,
Nature's embrace, a sweet caress,
A symphony of love, no less.

The Song of Crickets and Leaves

In the warm embrace of evening's light,
Crickets sing softly, a tranquil delight.
Leaves rustle gently, a whispering breeze,
Nature's sweet chorus, puts hearts at ease.

Moonlit shadows dance on the ground,
With every note, peace is found.
Stars begin to shimmer, one by one,
In this symphony, day is done.

The night unfolds with secrets untold,
Stories of magic, timeless and bold.
Each chirp and rustle, a delicate thread,
Weaving through darkness, where all fears shed.

Embrace the stillness, let worries cease,
In this twilight concert, find your peace.
Crickets and leaves in harmony blend,
A song of nature, without end.

Whimsy in the Glow of Celestial Nights

Under the vast and starry dome,
Whispers of dreams feel like home.
Each twinkle twirls, a dance divine,
In the glow of night, our spirits intertwine.

Colors of dusk paint the sky bright,
As laughter mingles with the night's light.
Cosmic wonders, a whimsical show,
Unfolding stories, soft and slow.

Clouds drift lazily, shadows of white,
Carrying wishes on wings of light.
With each star, a tale takes flight,
In the embrace of this magical night.

Gaze into the heavens, let your heart soar,
In the glow of the cosmos, forever explore.
Whimsy invites us, in its gentle sway,
To revel in moments that dance and play.

Shadows of Fairytales in Lush Darkness

In the depths of night, where dreams dwell,
Whispers of fairytales begin to swell.
Shadows flutter, like ghosts in disguise,
Weaving through stories, under starlit skies.

Mossy paths lead to forgotten lore,
With every step, we yearn for more.
Magic lingers where the wild things roam,
In the heart of darkness, we find our home.

Crimson roses bloom in the night air,
Guarded by secrets, both rich and rare.
Each petal holds a tale of old,
Of heroes and battles, and treasures untold.

Listen closely, the night has much to say,
In shadows of fairytales, we find our way.
Through the lush darkness, let spirits flow,
Where the essence of dreams continuously grow.

Ethereal Whispers Between Twinkling Stars

Beneath the canvas of a midnight hue,
Ethereal whispers speak soft and true.
Stars like candles, flicker in time,
Carrying secrets, in rhythm and rhyme.

Between them flows the essence of night,
A dance of light, pure and bright.
Each twinkle tells a tale of wonder,
A lullaby that calls from under.

Galaxies spin in a cosmic embrace,
Inviting hearts to join their grace.
Echoes of laughter, soft and clear,
Bring distant worlds ever so near.

In this celestial realm, we lose all fears,
Their whispers wrap us, like gentle tears.
In the vastness, our spirits ignite,
With ethereal whispers, we take flight.

Whispers of Light in the Sylvan Retreat

In the hush of green leaves sway,
Soft beams of sun gently play.
Fragrant blooms in quiet cheer,
Whispers of nature draw us near.

Beneath the boughs where shadows dance,
Time slows down in a hidden trance.
Sitting still, we breathe in deep,
Secrets the forest longs to keep.

The songbird's call, a tender sound,
Echoes through the thickets found.
A peace that seeps into our bones,
Fills our hearts, replaces stones.

Gentle streams weave paths of light,
Guiding us through the soft twilight.
Mossy banks, a velvet seat,
Where nature's pulse and magic meet.

As twilight wraps the world in gold,
Dreams begin to softly unfold.
Here in this sylvan retreat,
Light and whispers, bittersweet.

The Allure of the Enchanted Hour

Golden rays in the dusky sky,
Time stands still, the world a sigh.
Chasing shadows, dancing leaves,
In this moment, the heart believes.

The swallow's flight, a fleeting glance,
Invites the soul to join the dance.
Laughter rings in the evening breeze,
Fleeting time brings hearts to ease.

Twilight wraps the earth in grace,
Every moment a soft embrace.
Colors blend in a sweet display,
Painting dreams that drift away.

Where fireflies twinkle, secrets hide,
And hopes emerge, like stars, collide.
The forest whispers tales untold,
In the allure of twilight's hold.

As day departs, the magic grows,
In the enchanted hour, anything goes.
And in this silence, we find our way,
Every heartbeat leading us to stay.

Velvet Dreams Cradled in Nature's Hold

In the depths of vibrant green,
Dreams weave softly, pure and keen.
Hushed by the trees' soft caress,
Nature's hold, a sweet redress.

Stars awaken in the night,
Casting down their silvery light.
Whispers of the wind so clear,
Each moment feels like we are near.

Muffled sounds of rustling leaves,
Comfort wraps, like autumn eves.
Seasons change with tender grace,
Every heartbeat finds its place.

Moonlit reflections on the stream,
Lullabies within a dream.
Cradled softly, time stands still,
Nature's secrets, hearts to fill.

In this sanctuary, we belong,
Velvet dreams where souls grow strong.
Nestled deep in the quiet night,
Nature holds us, pure delight.

The Magic Between Glimpses of Light

Amidst the woods, the sunlight peeks,
In golden beams where silence speaks.
Whispers echo through ancient trees,
    Carried softly on a breeze.

Moments captured in time's embrace,
    Dancing shadows draw a trace.
Glimpses of magic softly blend,
As daylight meets the night's sweet end.

A flicker here, a shimmer there,
Sprinkling dreams like fragrant air.
Nature's pulse, a gentle sway,
Calls us forth to where we may.

Paths worn soft by wandering feet,
    Every turn a chance to meet.
Sunsets brush with hues divine,
Creating memories that intertwine.

In the spaces where light breaks through,
    We find the magic, pure and true.
Between the glimpses, hearts take flight,
    Drawing near to the endless light.

Radiance Between the Sorrel Leaves

Sunlight dances with gentle ease,
Whispers of gold in the soft breeze.
Sorrel leaves glimmer bright and green,
A canopy where dreams convene.

In the hush of the morning hour,
Nature sows its fragrant flower.
Every pulse, a sweet refrain,
Echoing through the grassy plain.

With dew drops like diamonds they shine,
A symphony of earth divine.
Beauty woven with tender care,
A secret realm, found everywhere.

As shadows linger, softly sway,
Time drifts by in its own way.
Each leaf a story, a life embraced,
In this tranquil, sacred place.

So pause a while, take it in,
Feel the warmth that lies within.
Between the sorrel, hope is found,
In gentle grace, life spins around.

Twilight's Caress on Celestial Hooves

The sky blushes, a canvas bright,
Hooves of stars take gentle flight.
Whispers of dusk on the silver grass,
Where dreams of night and day shall pass.

Upon the hills, shadows extend,
As moonbeams dance and softly bend.
Each hoofstep a promise unspoken,
A world where silence is unbroken.

Twilight's embrace, a lover's sigh,
Painting wonders across the sky.
Celestial steeds in a twilight race,
Our hearts follow in their gentle pace.

In this moment, time stands still,
A tranquil hush, a soft thrill.
Stars ripple like water's flow,
Twilight's caress, a sweet tableau.

So ride the night on luminous trails,
Where every heartbeat gently sails.
With celestial hooves that pave the way,
To dreams that dawn shall not delay.

Veils of Serenity in the Moonlit Forest

Moonlight drapes the forest deep,
A harmony, whispers that seep.
Veils of serenity softly fall,
Nature's balm, embracing all.

Among the trees, shadows weave,
In silence, the night takes leave.
Soft rustles tell a tale anew,
Of night's embrace in twilight hue.

The air is rich with fragrant dreams,
As silver beams guide gentle streams.
Crickets sing their lullabies clear,
Each note a blessing to the ear.

In this realm, the heart finds peace,
All worries fade, and troubles cease.
Veils of leaves in the moonlight swirl,
A sacred dance, a timeless twirl.

So wander deep, let your spirit soar,
Beneath the moon, forevermore.
In the forest, where dreams unite,
Serenity wraps you, pure and light.

Beneath the Glistening Canopy

Beneath the glistening canopy high,
Where whispers of nature laugh and sigh.
Leaves and branches, stories entwined,
A world of wonders, yet undefined.

In emerald hues, a tapestry grows,
Dancing sunlight, where the soft breeze blows.
Every flutter, a secret shared,
A glimpse of magic, peace declared.

Birds flit by on wings of grace,
Voices of joy in this sacred space.
Underneath, the earth breathes slow,
A lullaby, a gentle flow.

So let your worries drift away,
In the heart of nature, come what may.
Beneath the canopy, life unfolds,
A story of whispers, softly told.

So linger here, let time unwind,
In the warmth of the sun, solace find.
Beneath the glistening leaves above,
Feel the harmony, peace, and love.

Whispers of Enchanted Ferns

In the quiet glade, shadows sway,
Leaves embrace the light of day.
Gentle breezes softly sigh,
Nature's secrets float on high.

Ferns unfold their emerald grace,
Time dances in this sacred space.
Whispers linger, faint and sweet,
Life's melody; a soft heartbeat.

Moonlight bathes the forest floor,
Magic lingers at the door.
Echoes of the past resound,
In each curve, lost dreams are found.

Mossy carpets cradle sleep,
Among the roots, deep shadows creep.
Hope is woven in each thread,
In the stillness, dreams are fed.

Every rustle tells a tale,
In fragrant whispers, we set sail.
To enchanted realms, we entrust,
In nature's arms, we find our lust.

Shimmering Dreams Beneath the Stardust Canopy

A blanket of stars on velvet night,
Dreams take flight, spirits in sight.
In the hush of the cosmic sea,
Whispers of wonder set us free.

Moonbeams dance on the leaves above,
Where shadows twirl, and the night speaks love.
Moments flicker like fireflies bright,
In the dark, they share their light.

Beneath the boughs, secrets unfold,
Stories shared, both timid and bold.
A symphony of sighs and gleams,
In the night, we weave our dreams.

The breeze carries tales from afar,
Reflections glint like distant stars.
In this realm of magic and mirth,
We find our peace, our place of birth.

Together we dance, on starlit ground,
Where hearts align, and hope is found.
Beneath the canopy, fears disperse,
In shimmering dreams, the universe.

Secrets of the Verdant Veil

Beneath the leaves, a life concealed,
Whispers hidden, truths revealed.
In shadows deep, the heart learns to see,
Secrets tangled in a tapestry.

The forest breathes in timeless grace,
In emerald arms, we find our place.
Each rustle carries a story anew,
In the verdant veil, dreams break through.

Petals whisper in the morning dew,
Softly sharing the world's sweet view.
With every sigh, nature's song plays,
Echoing softly through the maze.

Sunlight pierces with golden rays,
Illuminating forgotten days.
In the warmth, roots intertwine,
Life and love in a grand design.

Among the ferns, we'll linger late,
In the embrace of our shared fate.
The secrets of the veil we'll keep,
In nature's arms, our souls will leap.

Twilight Dancers in the Glistening Grove

In twilight's arms, shadows take shape,
Silent steppers, a grand escape.
The grove alights with a golden hue,
Where every glance, feels like new.

Glistening droplets, like diamonds rare,
Adorn the leaves with tender care.
Night's soft blanket begins to fall,
Whispers of night, a gentle call.

Dancers twirl, free in the trance,
Under stars, they spin and prance.
In the moonlit glow, spirits sing,
Joy in motion, life takes wing.

With every breath, the magic grows,
In the grove, where wildness flows.
Embracing dreams in a sweet embrace,
With each beat, we find our place.

As evening fades, hearts brightly hum,
In nature's rhythm, we're all one.
Twilight's charm, a dance of light,
In the grove, we dance through the night.

Breaths of Mystery on Windy Nights

Whispers travel through the trees,
Carried softly on the breeze.
Stars twinkle in the velvet sky,
As shadows stretch and secrets lie.

Moonlight glimmers on the ground,
Where hidden tales are often found.
The chill air breathes a ghostly song,
In this place where spirits throng.

Branches sway to an ancient tune,
Beneath the watchful eye of the moon.
Every rustle tells a story old,
In hushed tones of silvers and gold.

Footsteps echo on winding paths,
Echoes of laughter from distant pasts.
Nature wraps her arms so tight,
In the embrace of windy night.

As dawn approaches, dreams take flight,
Fleeting shades retreat from light.
Yet in the stillness, one can find,
The mystery that fills the mind.

Serene Visions in the Depths of the Grove

Amidst the ferns, serenity flows,
A tranquil balm where stillness glows.
Dappled light through leaves will weave,
A tapestry that gives reprieve.

Gentle streams sing soft refrains,
Carving paths through earthy plains.
Each echo lingers, pure and bright,
Carrying whispers of sheer delight.

In shaded nooks, life hums and thrives,
Awakens dreams where magic dives.
Butterflies dance on petals' grace,
In this softly woven space.

The scent of pine, the earthy ground,
A symphony of peace resounds.
In every breath, a sacred hush,
Within the grove, the heart will rush.

As twilight falls, the world feels right,
Stars will gather, sharing light.
In the stillness, calm hearts find,
Serene visions, intertwined.

The Light that Dances in Shaded Nooks

Dappled sunbeams play a game,
In quiet corners, never the same.
Shadows waltz with golden rays,
A gentle dance that softly sways.

Leaves will shimmer, whisper sweet,
Where earth and sky and spirit meet.
The light casts colors, vivid, bold,
Unveiling stories yet untold.

In shaded nooks, a secret glow,
A treasure hidden, waiting slow.
Nature's canvas, bold and bright,
Reflects the magic of pure light.

Through twisted branches, light cascades,
Illuminating life in shades.
A moment's pause in time's embrace,
In every flicker, grace and space.

As day departs, dusk gently falls,
The last bright beams, a soft recall.
In these nooks, forever stays,
The light that dances in myriad ways.

Ethereal Threads of Nature's Quilt

In emerald fields where shadows play,
Threads of nature weave the day.
Petals brush the morning dew,
Creating patterns fresh and new.

Each leaf unfurls like whispered dreams,
Underneath the sun's warm beams.
In gentle winds, the fabric sways,
Crafting art in myriad ways.

Tangled roots embrace the earth,
Binding joy, binding worth.
The sky above in azure hue,
Stitches together moments true.

From mountain peaks to ocean deep,
Nature's quilt, a rhythm to keep.
Every color, every thread,
Tells the stories of those who've tread.

In quiet corners, life takes hold,
Page by page, the tale unfolds.
With every breath, we understand,
The ethereal threads that shape our land.

The Veiled Melodies of the Forest

In shadows deep, the whispers flow,
A gentle breeze, a softened glow.
Leaves dance lightly, secrets shared,
Nature's breath, a song declared.

Amidst the boughs, a voice is heard,
As if the trees had softly stirred.
Each note a tale of days gone by,
Beneath the still, enchanting sky.

The brook hums low, a rhythmic play,
Guiding footsteps on their way.
With every turn, a joy revealed,
The heart of earth, forever healed.

In twilight's hue, the nightingale sings,
Her melody to soften stings.
The veil of dusk, a cloak of dreams,
Where all is not as it first seems.

Lost in the woods, the mind takes flight,
With veiled tunes and flickering light.
A symphony of life unfolds,
In harmony, the forest holds.

Glimmers of Life in the Silence of the Wood

Amidst the trees, a stillness grows,
Where sunlight breaks and softly glows.
Life whispers here, in muted hues,
A world alive, the heart renews.

The fluttering leaves, a dance of fate,
Each rustling sound, a gentle trait.
In silence deep, small lives take hold,
The stories of the woods retold.

A deer slips by with grace and ease,
Among the trunks, she wanders free.
Her quiet steps, a fleeting grace,
In nature's arms, she finds her space.

Beneath tall oaks, the shadows play,
Where moments stretch and drift away.
Glimmers of life, both vast and small,
In forest whispers, we hear their call.

Each breath a pulse of secret dreams,
Reflecting glimmers, life redeems.
In every pause, the world aligns,
In silence rich, the heart designs.

Enchanted Epiphany Beneath the Leaves

Cloaked in shade, the magic stirs,
As sunlight filters through the slurs.
Each leaf a canvas, stories bare,
An epiphany hangs in the air.

Footfalls soft on mossy ground,
Where hidden wonders can be found.
In whispers past, the ancient trees,
Hold lessons in their creaking knees.

The vibrant hues of life unfold,
In nature's arms, everything's bold.
A moment's truth beneath the green,
Where worlds collide, and hearts careen.

Time suspended, a breath held tight,
In harmony with day and night.
Each thought a seed, a chance to grow,
Beneath the leaves, our spirits flow.

Embrace the space where magic lies,
In quietude, the spirit flies.
An epiphany for those who seek,
In nature's heart, the soul's mystique.

The Harmony of Spirits in the Wild

In twilight's glow, a dance begins,
Where earth and sky exchange their sins.
The whispering grass, a gentle sway,
Invites the spirits to play today.

The wind carries tales of those long gone,
In every gust, a heartfelt song.
Life pulses strong through roots and streams,
Where every shadow holds our dreams.

By starlit paths, we journey wide,
In nature's arms, there's nothing to hide.
The silence sings beneath the light,
In the harmony that feels so right.

Wolves call out as night descends,
A chorus strong that softly bends.
From mountain high to valley low,
The spirits resonate and flow.

In wild embrace, we find our place,
With every heartbeat, a gentle grace.
In the realm of earth, we intertwine,
A harmony of spirits aligns.

Ethereal Moments in the Hidden Wilds

In whispers soft, the forest breathes,
A dance of light through ancient trees.
Glimmers of magic, hushed and rare,
Nature's secrets linger in the air.

Beneath the canopy, shadows play,
A symphony of night fades into day.
With every step, the wild unfolds,
Stories of wonder waiting to be told.

The brook sings songs of timeless grace,
Each ripple captures nature's face.
Mossy carpets cushion every tread,
In the wild's embrace, we're gently led.

A deer appears, a fleeting muse,
In glades where gentle spirits cruise.
The scent of earth, both fresh and warm,
Invites the heart to weather any storm.

In these moments, time stands still,
Each breath a prayer, each heart a will.
Ethereal whispers guide our way,
Through hidden wilds where dreams hold sway.

Echoes of Enchantment Beneath Silver Leaves

Underneath the silver leaves,
Whispers weave through twilight eves.
Magic dances on the breeze,
Carried forth by secret trees.

Shadows cast from moonlit beams,
Reflect the glow of starlit dreams.
In every rustle, there's a tale,
An ageless song that will not pale.

The forest breathes in hushed delight,
As fireflies twinkle in the night.
Each step a note, each glance a chord,
Nature's hymn, a sweet reward.

Beneath the branches, stories sleep,
In solitude, their secrets keep.
Rays of silver paint the ground,
In this revered space, peace is found.

Echoes linger, soft and clear,
Every sigh, a memory near.
Beneath the silver leaves we stay,
Lost in wonder, night turns to day.

The Thread of Dreams in Nature's Hand

In twilight's glow, the path unfolds,
A tapestry of stories told.
Each leaf a memory, soft and grand,
The thread of dreams in nature's hand.

Upon the breeze, wishes glide,
Carried far like a soul's gentle ride.
The echoing whispers of the stream,
Weave through the fabric of every dream.

Where blossoms bow and colors blend,
The heart finds solace, spirits mend.
Verdant greens and skies so blue,
Nature's canvas, ever new.

In quiet corners, magic stirs,
Awakening wonder in secret purrs.
A butterfly flits, a spider spins,
In every moment, new life begins.

Threads entwine through day and night,
Binding beings in soft, pure light.
In nature's hand, our dreams expand,
A journey shared, a love unplanned.

Dawn's Promise in Velvet Thickets

In velvet thickets, dawn awakes,
Promises linger where silence breaks.
The horizon blushes in softest hue,
A tender moment, fresh and new.

Birdsongs ripple through the trees,
Nature's choir sings with ease.
Mist rises gently from the ground,
In this sacred space, beauty's found.

With every ray, the shadows flee,
Illuminating all that's meant to be.
Petals unfold, kissed by the sun,
In velvet thickets, life's begun.

Soft whispers call from deep within,
The promise of day, a gentle sin.
Each blade of grass, a story spun,
In dawn's embrace, we are all one.

Vibrant hues paint the waking land,
A dawn like this, forever grand.
In velvet thickets, hearts will sing,
For every morning brings new wings.

Secrets Written in Petal and Leaf

Whispers dwell in petals small,
Nature's tales that softly call.
Each leaf a secret, soft and bright,
Underneath the moon's sweet light.

In gardens where the shadows play,
Tender dreams weave night and day.
Colors dance in gentle waves,
Roots embrace what sunlight saves.

A fragrance lost on breezes sweet,
Echoes where the heart does meet.
In each bloom, a story glows,
The path of time in colors flows.

From every stem, a journey told,
In nature's arms, a treasure gold.
Secrets written, soft and dear,
In every petal, laughter near.

Among the leaves, a promise kept,
In the stillness, dreams are slept.
Listen close, the world will weave,
The secrets held in petal and leaf.

The Allure of Hidden Enchantment

Beneath the boughs where shadows blend,
Whispers linger, softly penned.
In twilight's glow, the magic stirs,
Where daylight fades, enchantment purrs.

Golden glows through emerald frames,
Nature's secrets, wild and untamed.
Each moment kissed by fleeting light,
A glimpse of dreams that dance in flight.

Where crystal streams in silence flow,
Hidden wonders start to grow.
Every rustle, every sigh,
Holds the truth of the evening sky.

Dew-kissed petals, stories weave,
In shadows deep, we dare believe.
The allure of night with all its charms,
Calls to wander, safe in its arms.

In every glen, a tale unfolds,
In whispered winds, enchantment holds.
Feel the pulse of the earth so near,
As hidden magic draws us here.

Radiant Paths Beneath Verdant Skies

A tapestry of life unfolds,
As sunlight spills in threads of gold.
Upon the path where blossoms sway,
Radiant dreams guide our way.

Through towering trees, the breezes sing,
Nature's chorus in everything.
With steps adorned in leafy grace,
We follow echoes of this place.

In meadows vast, where wildflowers bloom,
Their colors brush away the gloom.
Each petal whispers hope anew,
Beneath the skies, a deeper hue.

As shadows play on the forest floor,
The heartbeats quicken, yearning for more.
Together, we will roam and glide,
On radiant paths, with nature as guide.

With every turn, the spirit flies,
Onward through the verdant skies.
A journey rich with sights to see,
Where every moment is wild and free.

Nature's Lullaby in the Enchanted Wood

In the heart of the forest, whispers rise,
Nature sings beneath the skies.
With every breeze, a gentle tune,
Softly cradled by the moon.

Through emerald leaves, the shadows sway,
A lullaby that drifts away.
Crickets chirp in tender notes,
As the nightingale gently floats.

Each rustling branch holds dreams untold,
In the dark, a warmth unfolds.
In hush and stillness, the magic glows,
A symphony in nature's throes.

With every star, a story spins,
A calming peace as daylight thins.
In enchanted woods, we find our place,
Wrapped in nature's sweet embrace.

As slumber whispers from every tree,
Let the world fade, just you and me.
In the cradle of the night so good,
We'll dream to nature's lullaby in the wood.

Whispers in the Fernlight

In shadows deep, where ferns grow,
A gentle breeze begins to flow.
Soft whispers call, a secret song,
Inviting hearts to wander long.

Moonlit paths weave through the trees,
Carrying tales on the night breeze.
Glowing hints of magic's grace,
Embrace the wonder of this place.

Footsteps light on mossy ground,
Where hidden treasures can be found.
The stars above, in quiet gleam,
Guide our souls through twilight's dream.

In every leaf, a story spun,
Beneath the gaze of the evening sun.
Time stands still, as spirits play,
In the ferns, we lose our way.

So let the whispers softly call,
As we surrender, giving all.
For in this realm, we start anew,
With secrets shared, just me and you.

Secrets Beneath Celestial Canopies

Beneath the sky, where dreams unfold,
In whispers soft, the stars are told.
Canopies of night embrace the light,
While mysteries dance in silver flight.

Each twinkling star, a wish confined,
In hidden realms, their paths entwined.
The cosmos hums a soothing tune,
As night reveals the hidden moon.

Through branches thick, the shadows sway,
Where ancient secrets softly play.
A tapestry of life unspools,
With every breeze, the heart renews.

In twilight's glow, the stories blend,
Of love and loss, the journeys mend.
This sacred space, both vast and near,
In silence born, we find our cheer.

So gather close beneath the skies,
Where wisdom dwells and magic lies.
For here beneath the stars' bright gaze,
We uncover truth in gentle ways.

When Dreams Dance on Emerald Floors

On emerald floors where dreams ignite,
In twilight's hush and morning's light.
The dance of hope begins to rise,
Beneath the canopy of skies.

With every step, the world awakens,
In whispers sweet, the heart unshaken.
A joyful rhythm fills the air,
As petals fall, a fragrant prayer.

The streams beyond, they laugh and sing,
While nature's heart begins to spring.
In this enchanted, sacred space,
We find our truth, our saving grace.

Let shadows fade, let worries cease,
As dreams take flight and grant us peace.
In every twirl, in every glance,
We weave the fabric of our dance.

So join the chorus, feel it call,
Together we'll rise, together we'll fall.
For on these floors where dreams are sown,
We find a home in the unknown.

Enchantment in the Velvet Shadows

In velvet shadows, secrets sigh,
Where moonbeams brush the darkened sky.
A world unseen begins to gleam,
In soft embrace of twilight's dream.

Ethereal whispers fill the night,
In tender tones, they spark delight.
The air is thick with longing's grace,
As shadows fold, we find our place.

Each flicker of the starlit fire,
Ignites the heart with soft desire.
A dance of light, a fleeting chance,
As we too sway in night's romance.

With every breath, the magic swells,
In hidden spells where silence dwells.
For in the dark, we find our view,
The heart's true song, both old and new.

So linger here, in shadows deep,
Where dreams take flight, and lovers leap.
For in this world of soft embrace,
We find our truth, our sacred space.

Celestial Illusions Beneath Dappled Sunlight

In the forest's embrace, shadows play,
Golden rays dance, as leaves sway.
Whispers of dreams in the gentle breeze,
Nature's charm puts the heart at ease.

Petals claim the ground, soft and bright,
Colors blend, painting pure delight.
Each beam of light, a fleeting grace,
In the twilight's glow, we find our space.

Wandering souls on paths untold,
Stories linger, both new and old.
Among the branches, the secrets hide,
In rhythm with nature, we take our stride.

With every breath, the magic grows,
In silent wonders, the spirit knows.
Celestial dreams that call us near,
In this haven, all doubts disappear.

Beneath the sun's watchful, warm gaze,
We dance through life's enchanting maze.
As day gives way to the night's soft hum,
In nature's arms, we become one.

Dreamweaver's Secret in the Emerald Forest

Amongst the emerald, secrets reside,
A dreamweaver's touch, where shadows hide.
Ancient tales carve paths of lore,
In every whisper, a legend's core.

Glimmers of magic in the soft dew,
Under the canopy, where dreams come true.
Echoes of laughter, so sweet and clear,
Wrap around hearts, drawing them near.

The weaving of twilight, stars align,
In the hush of the night, the world is divine.
Every step taken, a spell is cast,
In the stillness of time, our spirits are vast.

In the rich tapestry of green and gold,
We find the treasures, stories unfold.
With every heartbeat, the forest sings,
Binding our souls to the joy that it brings.

Awake to the wonders that softly gleam,
In the heart of the forest, we live the dream.
Carried by the winds, free and fleet,
We dance with the stars, our souls complete.

Glistening Threads of Ephemeral Light

In twilight's embrace, the magic flows,
Glistening threads where the river glows.
Ephemeral moments, caught in flight,
Dancing on whispers, a beautiful sight.

Reflections ripple like tales untold,
In the fabric of time, shimmering gold.
Each heartbeat echoes, a timeless chime,
Weaving our stories, transcending time.

Through the strands of dusk, we wander free,
Drawn by the call of eternity.
Illusions of light on the forest floor,
A fleeting glimpse, forevermore.

Capturing dreams in the softest glow,
In the embrace of night, let love flow.
Every thread shines, a promise made,
In the tapestry of life, no fears invade.

Glistening moments, we hold them tight,
In the realm of dreams, we take flight.
Under the starlit sky's endless embrace,
We weave the night with a gentle grace.

A Serenade in the Heart of the Foliage

In the foliage deep, where the wild things sing,
A serenade blooms, like the joy of spring.
Leaves murmur softly, with secrets to share,
In this tranquil realm, dreams fill the air.

Nature's melody, with whispers of grace,
Guides us through moments, a timeless space.
The rustle of branches, a rhythm divine,
In this sacred haven, our hearts intertwine.

With every rustling leaf, a story unfolds,
Of worlds unseen and adventures bold.
In the twilight's glow, the magic ignites,
As shadows embrace the enchanting nights.

Draped in the silence, we find our way,
In the heart of the foliage, we long to stay.
The serenade calls, with a sweet refrain,
Binding us gently, like the softest rain.

Here in this sanctuary, time stands still,
With a heart open wide, we are free, we will.
In harmony's grip, we take our flight,
Lost in the serenade, embracing the night.

Echoes of the Ethereal Vale

In the valley where whispers cling,
Softly sings the breeze of spring,
Magic dances on the air,
Dreams unfurling everywhere.

Stone and shadow weave the night,
Stars awaken, shining bright,
In the stillness, secrets flow,
Echoes of the vale we know.

Misty paths and twilight glows,
Nature's beauty softly flows,
Hearts enchanted, lost in thought,
In this realm, all just forgot.

Every rustle, every sound,
Tells of wonders all around,
Silent tales of years gone by,
Underneath the endless sky.

Time can linger, slow and sweet,
In the vale, where souls may meet,
Gentle memories softly call,
Binding us within its thrall.

Luminescent Trails of Wandering Spirits

Through the night, a glow appears,
Leading whispers of our fears,
Stars above in silent flight,
Guiding lost souls through the light.

Footprints left on mossy ground,
Echoes of dreams that once were found,
Each warm glow a tale untold,
Casting stories, brave and bold.

In the stillness, spirits glide,
On the trails where hopes reside,
Light and shadow intertwine,
Wandering paths where hearts can shine.

Hidden truths in every beam,
Revealing wonders, fleeting dream,
In the night, we find our way,
Luminescent, come what may.

Trust the light that leads us home,
In the darkness, we will roam,
With each step the heart may sing,
To the dawn that whispers spring.

Beneath a Canopy of Wonder

In the forest, secrets gleam,
Under branches, we may dream,
Leaves like whispers, soft and green,
A hidden world, a magic scene.

Mossy carpets on the floor,
Nature's beauty, an open door,
Creatures watch with knowing eyes,
Beneath the vast and changing skies.

Each sunrise paints a new delight,
Coloring the day from night,
Dappled sunlight, shadows play,
In this realm, all fears decay.

Every moment holds a spark,
In the twinkle, find the mark,
Wonders whisper to the heart,
Beneath the canopy, art.

Journey onward, take the chance,
Feel the pulse of life's romance,
Open eyes and open soul,
In this wonder, we are whole.

Echoes of Forgotten Dreams in the Green Twilight

In the twilight, dreams take flight,
Echoes linger in the night,
Whispers of what could have been,
Fragrant thoughts of evergreen.

Beneath the boughs of ancient trees,
Secrets carried by the breeze,
Memories tucked in soft embrace,
Lost in time, a fleeting trace.

Silver shadows, soft and pale,
Carry stories on the trail,
Voices murmur from the past,
In this hour, shadows cast.

Swirling mist and quiet sighs,
Fragments of our long-lost ties,
In the green, where dreams remain,
Echoes whisper through the rain.

Let the twilight soothe the mind,
In these echoes, hope we find,
Every heart that dares to dream,
Lives forever in the stream.

Enigmas in the Brume of Twilight

Whispers dance in fading light,
Secrets held in gentle night.
Shapes that flicker, shadows play,
Mysteries of the ending day.

Veils of mist, they softly creep,
In the silence, secrets seep.
Hidden paths in twilight's hue,
Guide the heart to something new.

A lantern glows far from sight,
Echoes call in sweet twilight.
Every step a story told,
Of dreams woven, brave and bold.

In the brume where visions meld,
Time stands still as fear is quelled.
Dance of fate in shadows spun,
Beneath the watchful, fading sun.

What lies beyond the spectral veil?
A tale of wonder, love, and frail.
For in the twilight's tender grace,
Enigmas thrive in their embrace.

The Glint of Stars in Nature's Embrace

Among the trees, stars softly gleam,
Whispers shared in a silver dream.
A flicker here, a sparkle there,
Nature's charm beyond compare.

Petals shine with dewdrop light,
Melodies flow through the night.
Crickets sing as shadows blend,
In a world where night transcends.

Each twinkle tells a silent tale,
Of moonlit paths and gentle gale.
Threads of starlight weave through time,
In nature's heart, a perfect rhyme.

Beneath the heavens, dreams take flight,
In the embrace of tranquil night.
A cosmic dance, a celestial hum,
Life's secrets whispered, softly come.

Stars like gems on velvet skies,
Guide the lost with tranquil sighs.
In nature's cradle, peace abounds,
As glints of stars weave brighter bounds.

Riddles of Light and Shadow

Light and shadow intertwine,
Crafting tales both dark and fine.
Figures move in soft embrace,
Riddles drawn in time and space.

Sunlight kisses the forest's brow,
Painting dreams, a solemn vow.
Yet in the dark, secrets rustle,
Mysteries in friendly tussle.

Whispers breeze through sunlit glades,
Where every heartbeat softly fades.
Echoes of a world unknown,
In light's grip, shadows have grown.

Glimmers flash, a curious sight,
In the dance of day and night.
Riddles spun, both sweet and dire,
In the heart of nature's fire.

Within the realms where secrets lie,
The moon's soft gaze, a watchful eye.
Riddles echo, stories blend,
In light and shadow, fears transcend.

Seraphic Shadows on the Forest Floor

In woods where sunlight softly breathes,
Seraphic shadows weave through leaves.
A dance of light amidst the green,
Where nature's magic can be seen.

Beneath the branches, whispers swirl,
Every shadow, a hidden pearl.
Crimson blooms and emerald hues,
Seraphic grace in morning's muse.

Footsteps fall on ancient ground,
Where echoes of the past resound.
In every glade and fragrant nook,
Seraphs wander, their secrets took.

Light cascades like liquid gold,
Tales of wisdom, gently told.
Through the shadows, hearts align,
In the forest where spirits shine.

Beneath the leaves, a world unfolds,
In seraphic shades, life beholds.
Each breath a note in nature's song,
In the forest, we all belong.

Pastel Dreams in the Enchanted Meadow

Soft hues drift in the twilight sky,
Whispers of petals begin to sigh.
Colors dance in a gentle breeze,
Nature's canvas, a heart at ease.

Shadows play where the wildflowers grow,
A symphony sweet, in soft undertow.
Each blade of grass tells a story sweet,
As evening's glow makes the day retreat.

Beneath the stars, dreams gently unfold,
In the meadow, where secrets are told.
Pastels weave through the night so grand,
Enchanting moments, like grains of sand.

Clouds drift by in colors of cream,
Filling the hearts with a silent dream.
By the brook where the nightbirds sing,
Pastel dreams take to gentle wing.

At dawn's first light, a new song starts,
The meadow whispers to all our hearts.
With every hue and the softest light,
Magic lives where dreams take flight.

The Glimmering Realm of Elusive Creatures

In shadows deep, where the lost ones roam,
Whispers of magic call them home.
Glimmers twinkle in the silent night,
Elusive creatures, a wondrous sight.

They flit between the trees with grace,
Ghostly forms in a hidden place.
With every rustle, a kaleidoscope,
Hearts entwined in a thread of hope.

Moonbeams shimmer on their flowing trails,
As soft as the wind, like forgotten tales.
They dance in patterns no eye can see,
In the glimmering realm, wild and free.

A flicker here, a shimmer there,
Illusions weave in the midnight air.
Trust the whispers, let your heart believe,
In the realm where dreams weave and cleave.

Through emerald leaves, their laughter flows,
In the cool of night, while the starlight glows.
These creatures dwell beyond the known,
In a realm where true magic is sown.

Tales Woven in the Misty Undergrowth

Softly spoken in the morning haze,
Whispers of stories from ancient days.
Misty tendrils embrace the ground,
In the undergrowth, lost tales abound.

Each leaf a page, each branch a line,
Woven tales shimmering, divine.
Echoing softly through the tangled roots,
Forgotten secrets, in nature's boots.

As dew drops cling to the fragile blooms,
The forest breathes with its silent tunes.
Voices of old in the rustling leaves,
In the misty gloom, the heart believes.

Fables of creatures hidden from sight,
Spinning their webs in the soft twilight.
Nature's lore wrapped in fragrant air,
In the undergrowth, dreams lay bare.

Through the embrace of the morning light,
Every corner flourishes in sight.
In the gentle hush, wisdom is found,
Tales woven deep in the misty ground.

Spirals of Light Through the Forest Floor

Dappled sunlight breaks through the trees,
Whispering secrets in the gentle breeze.
Spirals of light dance upon the ground,
A magic carpet in colors profound.

The forest hums with a life untamed,
Where shadows play and hopes are named.
Each ray of sun a golden thread,
Through ancient woods where the wild things tread.

Mushrooms peek from their emerald beds,
Tiny worlds where adventure spreads.
In every twist, a story gleams,
Of forgotten paths and silver dreams.

Beneath the canopy, a labyrinth grows,
In spirals of light, where the river flows.
Each footstep taken, a spell is cast,
In the heart of the woods, forever vast.

Echoes of laughter, the rustle of leaves,
In this tapestry, the heart believes.
As twilight falls, the magic soars,
In spirals of light, through the forest floors.

Moonlit Dreams on Fern-cloaked Floors

Whispers of night in gentle embrace,
Fern-cloaked floors, a secret place.
Moonlight dances, casting its glow,
Where dreams awaken, soft and slow.

Shadows move with a silken grace,
Each step taken, a soft trace.
In this realm of the serene,
Stars above like pearls agleam.

A lullaby sung by whispering trees,
Carried softly on the night breeze.
Echoes of laughter drift through the air,
As ghosts of the past linger there.

Within the silence, a heartbeat thrums,
Nature's symphony, sweetly it hums.
Fingers of light caress the ground,
In this sanctuary, peace is found.

So let the night weave its mystic thread,
In moonlit dreams, where hope is bred.
With fern-cloaked floors beneath our feet,
Adventure awaits, so wild and sweet.

The Symphony of Nature's Silhouettes

In twilight's arms, the world transforms,
Nature's silhouettes take new forms.
Branches sway in a tender sigh,
As fireflies dance, flitting by.

Mountains stand, bold and grand,
Guarding secrets of this land.
Rivers murmur, a soothing sound,
In harmony with the earth, profound.

Night wraps close, a velvet cloak,
Every whisper a tale bespoke.
Beneath the stars, the earth is bare,
Each silhouette a love affair.

In the stillness, spirits roam,
Finding solace far from home.
Nature sings a timeless song,
In this world where we belong.

Let us listen to the night's decree,
In nature's arms, we are truly free.
A symphony of light and shadow,
In the dance of life, gently we follow.

Luminescence in the Veil of Dreams

A soft glow blankets the sea of night,
Whispers of dreams take gentle flight.
In the veil where the shadows play,
Hope is born as night meets day.

Stars like pearls hang in the sky,
Guiding lost souls from way up high.
In the silence, magic stirs,
As each heartbeat softly purrs.

Veils of mist, a soft embrace,
Shrouding the world in a tender grace.
In the depths of slumber we find,
The luminescence of the mind.

With every dream, a story we weave,
In this tapestry we all believe.
In the glow of the night's soft beam,
We dance our way through every dream.

Secrets Beneath the Castle of Leaves

In the forest deep, a castle stands,
Built by nature's unseen hands.
Leaves whisper secrets on the breeze,
Tales of travelers lost with ease.

Ancient roots weave stories old,
In shadows cast, treasures untold.
Beneath the layers, secrets lie,
Waiting beneath the watchful sky.

Branches twist like fingers of fate,
Guarding places that lie in wait.
Each rustle evokes a ghostly sigh,
In the castle where dreams never die.

In nature's heart, time drifts slow,
As hidden wonders start to glow.
With every whisper, a truth unfolds,
In the forest's embrace, life never grows old.

So wander through this enchanted maze,
Where magic lingers in sunlit rays.
Beneath the castle of leaves, we roam,
Finding the secrets that guide us home.

Luminous Echoes of Enchanted Realms

In realms where shadows weave and glow,
Whispers of magic begin to flow.
Starlight dances on the forest floor,
A symphony of dreams forevermore.

Chasing the beams that shimmer bright,
Guided by the moon's gentle light.
Echoes of laughter linger in the air,
As secrets unfold without a care.

Mysteries hidden beneath the trees,
Invite wandering souls with the breeze.
A tapestry woven of night and day,
In enchanted realms where spirits play.

The pulse of the earth beats steady and true,
Every heartbeat sings a song anew.
Luminous echoes call out our names,
Drawing us deeper into their games.

Together we dance on this woven thread,
With stories of magic that never shred.
Luminous echoes resound through the night,
In the heart of the realms, pure delight.

Beneath the Woven Tapestry of Twilight

Underneath the twilight's veil,
The sky blushing with secrets to unveil.
Stars emerge in a silent embrace,
As day surrenders to night's gentle grace.

Whispers of dawn linger in the air,
Carried softly without a care.
Cascading colors paint the skies,
A woven tapestry where beauty lies.

Night blooms with a fragrant, soft sigh,
Casting dreams as the world goes by.
Beneath this cloak of twilight's charm,
Every shadow holds a subtle calm.

In every star, a story waits,
To stir the dreams behind celestial gates.
The night cradles wishes, pure and bright,
Beneath the woven tapestry of twilight.

Moments suspended in quiet delight,
Echo through the stillness of the night.
As dawn approaches, the world will wake,
Beneath this tapestry, hearts won't break.

Breath of the Otherworldly Grove

In the grove where the ancients reside,
Breath of magic flows like a tide.
Rustling leaves share secrets untold,
Wrapped in whispers of mystical gold.

Mossy carpets cradle weary feet,
Where shadows and light softly meet.
The pulse of the earth, a soothing hum,
Invites you to listen, inviting to come.

Each fluttering wing tells a tale,
Of wanderers lost on a gentle trail.
A world unseen dances in view,
Under the gaze of a sky so blue.

In every breath, a promise unfolds,
A bond with nature that forever holds.
The otherworld calls with a gentle plea,
To find your spirit, to set it free.

Embrace the magic in every sigh,
In the grove where dreams never die.
With each heartbeat, the grove will grow,
Breath of otherworldly wonders flow.

Shimmering Trails Beneath Ancient Boughs

Beneath the ancient, towering trees,
Shimmering trails beckon with ease.
Footprints left in the silvery dew,
Guide the wanderer to realms anew.

The branches whisper tales of yore,
As sunlight dapples the forest floor.
Each step reveals a magic unseen,
In the heart of nature, serene and keen.

A dance of shadows, a play of light,
Drawing forth dreams that take flight.
Beneath the boughs where secrets thrive,
Shimmering trails keep the magic alive.

With every breath, the earth's heartbeat calls,
In this elixir where wonder enthralls.
Ancient boughs cradle time and space,
Shimmering trails, an embrace of grace.

So wander long through this sacred place,
Where the spirit of nature reveals its face.
In the woods' embrace, let your soul gleam,
On shimmering trails, we chase the dream.

Beneath the Celestial Tapestry

Stars shimmer like diamonds bright,
Woven tales of the endless night.
Whispers dance on the velvet sky,
Dreams take wing, they learn to fly.

Galaxies spin in a cosmic ballet,
Time drifts gently, night turns to day.
Under this dome, hearts intertwine,
Each pulse a rhythm, a love divine.

Comets streak, leaving trails of fire,
Fleeting moments, our souls aspire.
In the cool night, we share our fears,
Beneath the watchful, starlit peers.

Moonbeams whisper secrets untold,
A tapestry of warmth, a sight to behold.
In silence, connection draws us near,
Beneath the cosmos, all is clear.

In this expanse, the infinite calls,
Under the sky, love conquers all.
Let the night cradle us in its might,
Beneath the celestial, we find our light.

Luminous Echoes in the Hidden Glade

In a forest deep where shadows play,
Soft whispers glimmer throughout the day.
Luminous echoes weave through the trees,
Carried on the backs of a gentle breeze.

Moss carpets the earth like a velvet dream,
Rivers of light in the sun's warm beam.
Creatures of magic flit to and fro,
In this hidden glade, secrets bestow.

Ferns sway lightly to nature's tune,
Dancing sparks beneath the watchful moon.
Every rustle, each chirp a song,
Welcoming travelers who wander along.

Soft shadows cradle the heart's delight,
Guiding lost souls through the soft twilight.
Captivated by beauty, time drifts away,
In luminous echoes, we long to stay.

As day turns to night, stars softly gleam,
Embraced in peace, we follow the dream.
In this hidden glade, life paints its art,
Threads of enchantment woven in the heart.

Mysteries of the Emerald Glow

Deep in the woods, a soft emerald light,
Whispers of magic fill the cool night.
Beneath the boughs, secrets unfold,
Tales of wonder, enchantments told.

Crickets serenade under the stars,
Nature's symphony, in rhythm, it jars.
Misty tendrils, like dreams in the air,
Draw us closer, allure us to dare.

Twilight's embrace brings shadows alive,
Where the heart learns and wild spirits thrive.
Each rustle and murmur will leave a trace,
Mysteries shimmer in this embrace.

Fireflies linger, painting the night,
Guiding us gently with flickers of light.
An invitation to worlds yet unseen,
Where the magic of life greets our keen.

In this emerald glow, fear melts away,
Wrapped in the night, we dream and we sway.
Lost in the wonder, we find our own way,
In mysteries whispered, forever we stay.

Enchanted Shadows in Moonlit Thickets

In the thick of the woods, shadows dance low,
Bathed in the silver moon's gentle glow.
Mysteries written in fleeting light,
Enchanted whispers of the night.

Branches weave tales of shadows and dreams,
Nature's secrets flow like soft streams.
Under the arch of stars, we roam,
Lost in the stillness, we find our home.

Every step soft on the cool, wet ground,
Magic awakens, in silence, profound.
With each heartbeat, the forest sighs,
In moonlit thickets, where enchantment lies.

Luna's glow casts a spell on the trees,
Caressing the night with a gentle breeze.
Here in the thicket, the world stands still,
Following whispers, we bend to its will.

In this wonder, shadows reveal,
A symphony of dreams that we can feel.
Through enchanted forests, side by side,
In moonlit thickets, our spirits bide.

www.ingramcontent.com/pod-product-compliance
Ingram Content Group UK Ltd.
Pitfield, Milton Keynes, MK11 3LW, UK
UKHW021433160125
4146UKWH00006B/74